MUSLIMS IN AMERICA

Seven Centuries of History

(1312-2000)

Collections and Stories of American Muslims

Amir Nashid Ali Muhammad

D0188399

amana publications
Beltsville, MD

First Edition (1998/1418 AH)
Second Edition (2001/1421 AH)
Third Edition (2003/1424 AH)

© 1998, 2001 by Amir N. Muhammad

amana publications
10710 Tucker Street
Beltsville, Maryland 20705-2223 USA
Tel: (301)595-5777 Fax: (301)595-5888
E-mail: amana@igprinting.com
Website: www.amana-publications.com

Library of Congress Catalogue-in-Publication Data
Muhammad, Amir N. (Amir Nashid)
Muslims in America : seven centuries of history, 1312–2000 : collections and stories of American Muslims / Amir Nashid Ali Muhammad.–2nd ed.
p. cm.
Includes biliographical references.
ISBN 0–915957–75–2
1. Islam–United States–History. 2. Muslims–United States--History. 3. Black Muslims--United States--History. 4. African Americans–Religion–History.

BP67.U6 M84 2001
297'.0973–dc21

2001022274

Printed in the United States of America by
International Graphics
10710 Tucker Street
Beltsville, Maryland 20705-2223 USA
Tel: (301) 595-5999 Fax: (301) 595-5888
E-mail: ig@igprinting.com

CONTENTS

Foreword

American Muslims are now a part of the cultural landscape of the United States of America. Their numbers have grown significantly over the last four decades. Because of this growing visibility and self-confidence, many of them with the ability to do research have begun to publish works designed to increase the knowledge of the average American about the history and development of Islam in the United States. As a result, a growing body of literature on American Muslims is developing throughout the country. The publication in your hand is one of the latest in the expanding number of printed works seeking a respectable place in the library of the reading American public.

The material presented within this book is the fruit of many hours of tedious research in libraries and other places where researchers could secure materials that can shed light on the young Muslim community and in the United States. Mr. Muhammad has spent time talking to a variety of Muslims about this project and his work should be seen as one of the pioneering efforts to fill gaps in the historical record of our community. As a brick in the edifice of American Muslim scholarship, this work is recommended to Muslims and non-Muslims who are genuinely interested in knowing how Muslims came to the U.S. and what the major historical events are that identify the birth and development of this community of believers.

The work does not claim to be exhaustive; however, one can say that its contribution will be judged not only for the dates it provides but also for the chronology of events that give significance and meaning to Muslim life and history on this continent. Those who take time to go over it will walk away enriched by its contents.

Sulayman S. Nyang, Ph.D.
Professor of African Studies
Howard University

Message from the President of Collections and Stories of American Muslims (CSAM)

Muslims in America: Seven Centuries of History was published to help educate the American public, as well as the global community, of America's Islamic history and contributions. This collection of history is the frame work for building a museum of Muslim Americans.

In it, one will find many fascinating stories and insightful historical events. The story of Job Ibn Solomon Jallo will remind one of the Quran and Bible story of prophet Job's life and struggles. It will make many Muslims and Americans proud to know that there were some Muslims who helped defend the country in the War of 1812 against the British.

The story of Ben Ali (Bu Allah: Abdullah) Bilali, the slave from Georgia will make one feel proud of the Islamic community he developed in Georgia as a slave in the 1800s and his determination to hold on to his Islamic life no matter what his condition and circumstances were. His story has many similarities of the life of Bilal Ibn Rabah, who lived during the life time of the prophet (swa). Both Bilal's, showed strength and courage in their Islamic values and religion during desperate and oppressive times.

Collections and Stories of American Muslims, Inc. (CSAM) was created in 1996 to establish an Islamic traveling exhibition, archives, and Museum in America and for abroad. The exhibit reflects America's Islamic heritage and history.

CSAM continues to seek information, material, artifacts, stories, and donations for the development of an Muslim American Islamic museum.

You can contact us at:

Collections and Stories of American Muslims

2524 Elvans Road
Washington, D.C. 20020-3508
(202) 678-6906
E-mail amirmuhammad@juno.com

This book was published with a grant from the American Muslim Foundation, Washington DC
Abdul-Hakeem Muhammad

Bismi-llah (In the Name of God)

Letter from the Director of Collections and Stories of American Muslims (CSAM)

When my husband told me he was going to write a book about American Muslims, highlighting the experiences of slaves who were Muslims, I was overwhelmed and didn't quite feel his passion; I had already read many books written about Muslims and Muslim slaves. However, with his perseverance, constant researching, re-editing, rewriting, and probing, it became evident that his work would be a very special and inclusive historical text. You can definitely feel his passion in this book.

As this is the second edition, I know that in time more historical facts will be added and more research will be done to further enhance it. Books are constantly being written by scholars around the world and Amir has proven himself to be a scholar in his own right. I am certain his book will be given the recognition it deserves.

As Collections and Stories of American Muslims (traveling exhibition and archives) emerges as a forthright cultural and historical institution, *Muslims in America: Seven Centuries of History* (1312–1997) sets the proper tone for our endeavors. This book is an important step toward the further understanding of and appreciation for the Islamic history of Muslims in America.

Habeebah D. Muhammad
Director, CSAM

Introduction

In the 60s during the Civil Rights Movement, Muslims in the Nation of Islam and others had an impact on the Black consciousness movements.

During the 1970s, Muslims and Islam had an impact on America's music culture with the message songs of the Philadelphia Sound, with black pride and dignity from personalities such as Muhammad Ali, and with Alex Haley's book *Roots: The Saga of an American Family*. The Islamic life of Kunte Kinte motivated many Americans to research their genealogical history. In the late 70s Muslims once again had an influence and impact on the cultural identity of African Americans from being known as Blacks to African Americans.

I pray you will enjoy the rich message and knowledge of America's Islamic history in the next few pages. And as more information emerges we will, *insha Allah* (God willing), continue to publish and evolve the Collections and Stories of American Muslims' museum and traveling exhibit.

I thank Allah (God) for His blessings and mercy. I would like to thank my parent's Herbert and Mable West for their love and support. On my father's side through his bloodline, my direct 7th generation ancestor from Africa,

Clara Higgenbotham, was found in the US 1870 census. She was born in West Africa in 1793 and then enslaved sometime between 1815 and 1817 in Brunswick, Georgia. In 1870, one of Clara's daughters was living with her, named Amry Bakr, a very familiar Islamic name. Clara lived during the same time period and about 10 minutes away from the same area as Salih Bilali, one of the enslaved Muslims highlighted in my book.

It was through my genealogical research, discovering my African ancestor, that I became motivated and driven to study the Islamic history of America.

Lastly, I would like to thank my wife Habeebah Muhammad, for without her dedication and support this work could not have been possible. I would also like to thank the staff of the AMC (American Muslim Council)— Fahim Abdul-Hadi, Hanan Williams, and Suraiya Hassan—for the time and energy they spent editing.

Amir N. Muhammad
Author and Researcher

EARLY HISTORICAL MOMENTS
(1312–1600)

In **1312,** African Muslims arrived in the Gulf of Mexico for exploration of the American interior using the Mississippi River as their access route. These Muslim explorers were from Mali and other parts of West Africa. The brother of Mansa Musa, Abubakari, was one of the first to set sail to America from Africa.

In **1492,** when Christopher Columbus arrived in the New World, he was strongly influenced by the geography of the 13th-century Arab scholar, Al-Idrissi, who served as an adviser to King Roger of Sicily. Columbus had with him a copy of Al-Idrissi's works mentioning the discovery of a new continent by eight Muslim explorers. He also had some Muslim crew members with him for translation and other services.

Columbus had two captains of Muslim origin during his first voyage, one named Martin Alonso Pinzon the captain of the Pinta, and his brother Vicente Yanex Pinzon the captain of the Nina. They were wealthy expert ship outfitters who helped organize Columbus' expedition and repaired the flagship Santa Maria. The Pinzon family was related to Abuzayan Muhammad III, the Moroccan Sultan of the Marinid Dynasty (1196–1465).

October 21, 1492, Columbus admitted in his papers that while his ship was sailing near Gibara on the northeast coast of Cuba, he saw a Mosque on the top of a beautiful mountain. Ruins of Mosques and minarets with inscriptions of Qur'anic verses have been discovered in Cuba, Mexico, Texas, and Nevada.

In Dr. Barry Fell's book *Saga America,* he reports that the southwest Pima people possessed a vocabulary which contained words of Arabic origin. Dr. Fell also reports that in Inyo County, California, there exits an early rock carving which stated in Arabic: "Yasus ben Maria" ("Jesus, Son of Mary"). Dr. Fell discovered the existence of schools in Nevada, Colorado, and New Mexico.

In **1527,** the Spanish explorer Panfilo de Narva'ez left Spain for the Americas. In his fleet he had five ships and six hundred people in his company. The expedition met with many hardships. Several ships were destroyed by a West Indies hurricane and a group of Indians killed a large number of the remaining members of the party. Afterward, when only a few members of the expedition were left, Cabeza de Vaca, the former treasurer of Narva'ez took up the leadership of the remaining members of the party with Estevanico being among them.

Estevanico was called an Arab Negro, a Muslim who came from Azamore on the Atlantic Coast of Morocco. He was among the first two persons to reach the west coast of Mexico in an exploring overland expedition from Florida to the Pacific Coast. It's reported that Estevanico acted as a guide and it took them nine years to reach Mexico City where they told stories of their travels.

In **1538**, Estevanico lead an expedition from Mexico with Friar Marco, in search of the fabled Seven Cities of

Cibolia, in which time he discovered Arizona and New Mexico. He was the first member of a different race reported to have visited the North Mexican Pueblos. He was killed in the city of Cibolia, one of the Seven Cities of the Zuni Indians, which is now New Mexico. Friar Marco, while following Estevanico's trail to Cibolia, learned of his murder from an Indian messenger.

In **1539,** Estevanico was one of the first of three Americans to cross this continent. At least two states owe their beginning to this Muslim, Arizona and New Mexico.

From **1566** to **1587,** Spain kept and maintained a military outpost and settlement called Santa Elena on the southern tip of Parris Island, South Carolina. Portuguese were known to be among the Spaniards at Santa Elena. Today the Island is known as Saint Helena, South Carolina where they have an annual Gullah festival.

In Spain in **1568,** the Alpujarra uprising of the Moriscos (Muslims' who were forcibly converted to Catholicism) gave cause to another wave of Portuguese Moriscos to leave Spain.

In **1600,** the first Melungeons were reported in the southern Appalachian valleys. As English and Scotch-Irish settlers moved in, they pushed the Melungeons into the mountains of North Carolina, and into Tennessee, Kentucky, and Virginia. The Melungeons were the first people, aside from Native Americans to penetrate so deeply into the Appalachian region. Many of the Melungeons were of primarily Portuguese ancestry, with North African and Indian traits. Among the early

5

Portuguese were the Moriscos of Spain who were escaping persecution. Today there are still some Melungeons living secretively and many have assimilated into the American culture.

The Melungeons operated rich silver mines in the area of Straight Creek in the Cumberland Plateau, near Pineville, Kentucky. They minted silver coins in the area for their own use. By the time Kentucky joined the Union and became a Commonwealth, the independent secretive life of the Melungeons came to an end.

In **1600**, The Indians told Jamestown residents that with only a six-day walk to the west, there were "people like you," who wore their hair short and built log houses.

In **1639**, The First black recorded by name on the Delmarva Peninsula was called Anthony. He was delivered near present day Wilmington. He was often described as "an Angoler or Moor," and called "Blackamoor." (From the "Delaware's Forgotten Folk" The Story of the Moors & Nanticokes by C.A. Weslager)

In **1654**, English explorers from Jamestown reported finding a colony of bearded people "Moors" wearing European clothing, living in cabins, engaging in mining, smelting silver, and dropping to their knees to pray many times daily in the mountains of what is now, North Carolina.

In **1670**, Virginia General Assembly 1670 Act declared who will be slaves, excluding Turks & Moors, whose countries were in amity with the King of England. (Page

491 of Virginia General Assembly 1733 and 1752 records.)

In **1684**, Moors are reported to have arrived in Delaware near Dover, and in Southern New Jersey near Bridgeton.

History shows that Muslims came to the Americas in four different waves, the first as explorers, then those fleeing the Spanish Inquisition, during the Barbary Coast Wars and the enslavement of Africans, and by immigration starting in the mid-to-late 1870s.

The descendants of some of the early Muslim visitors of North America are members in many of our present day Indian tribes. Some of the tribes are the Alibamu tribe of Alabama, the Apaches, Anasazi, Arawak, Arikana, the Black Indians of the Schuylkill river area in New York, the Cherokees, Creeks, Makkahs, Mahigans, Mohanets, Mohegans, Nanticokes, Seminoles, Zulus, and the Zuni.

The Moors were inhabitants of Delaware near Dover, and of Southern New Jersey near Bridgeton, and in parts of Southern Maryland; the Melungeons of Tennessee and Virginia; the Guineas of West Virginia; the Clappers of New York; the Turks of South Carolina; and the Laster Tribe near Hertford, NC. It is reported that the Laster Tribe were descendants from a Moorish captain who married a white woman and settled in the area.

Many African Americans are descendants of Muslims who came to America's shores after being enslaved in West Africa and some from losing in the Barbary Coast Wars in North Africa.

Suggested Reading

Africa and the Discovery of America by Leo Wiener
World's Great Men of Color by J.A. Rogers
They Came Before Columbus by Ivan Van Sertima
African Presence in Early America by Ivan Van Sertima

HISTORICAL MOMENTS OF THE 1700s

The 1700s brings into focus a few Muslim scholars being enslaved in America, Muslims fighting in America's Revolutionary War, Muslims petitioning the government for their freedom and winning, Muslim names starting to appear in runaway slave advertisements, and America developing international relationships with Muslim countries.

The Climate of the 1700s

There were 59,000 free Blacks in the United States at the time of the first decennial census in 1790. Slightly more than 27,000 were in the Northern states and 32,000 were in the Southern states.

At least 5 Muslims who were enslaved and brought to America in the 1700s became famous: Ayub (Job) ibn Dijallo (1730), Lamine Jay (1730), Kunta Kinte (1767), Abrahim Abdul Rahman ibn Sori (1788), and Yarrow Marmood (1796).

In the early 1700s we find notes in New England history of African Americans practicing different Islamic customs, and many women with the name Hagar which derives from the name Hajar, the mother of Ishmael, prophet Ibrahim's son. In Islamic tradition Hajar is buried by the well of Zamzam in Mecca, Saudi Arabia.

Samples of some of the concerns European Americans had of some African Americans practices and customs:

> In **1713**, the Reverend John Sharpe reported from New York the existence of what he called "Negro marriages," he described a situation familiar to New Englanders. The marriages of the blacks, he explained, "are performed by mutual consent without the blessing of the Church." Some slaves, he went on, were kept from Christian marriage "because of polygamy contracted before baptism where none or neither of the wives will accept a divorce." (From Black Kings and Governors of New England.)

> In **1719,** The Reverend Peter Thatcher of Milton, Massachusetts complained about his slave woman Hagar's sexual life. She was a slave who was married to Sambo, a slave of Mr. Brightman of Boston, in 1716. She apparently had another child after Sambo's death or departure from the area by 1719. Hagar had three children Sambo, Jimmie, and Hagar. (From Black Kings and Governors of New England.)

By **1730** the history of Muslims in America began to unfold.

11

In **1730** Lamine Jay came from Futa-Toro, Senegal. He was captured along with Job ibn Soliman ibn Dijallo (Jallo) trading on the lower part of the Gambia river. Lamine was also brought to Annapolis, Maryland where he became known as a Linguist. In less than five years Jay was able to win his freedom and return home with the help of his friend Job.

In **1741** in New York City, three Moorish crew members of a captured Spanish ship were sold into bondage and protested their condition, swearing revenge. After several fires flared across town during March and April of 1742, hysterical residents feared that a slave revolt was imminent and suspected that the Spanish Negroes "Moors" were deeply concerned and active in the business. The episode ended with the public executions of twenty-three people and the exile of seventy-one others. (From the Seaport New York's History Magazine.)

Photo courtesy of Amherst College.

In **1730** Ayuba (Job) Suleiman Dijallo, a well-educated Muslim merchant was kidnaped and enslaved from 1730–1733. Job ibn Solomon Dijallo (Jallo) came from Bundu, Senegal. He was captured in 1730 in Gambia and brought to Annapolis, MD in 1731, where he was delivered to a Mr. V. Denton, factor to Mr. Hunt. Mr. Denton sold Job to Mr. Alexander Tolsey of Kent Island in Maryland.

Job was a Fulani who lived near the banks of the Gambia river in Senegal. Job was one of the first Muslims written

12

about in America. In Maryland Job wrote a letter to his father, which came to the attention of James Oglethorpe, the founder of Georgia, who helped purchase his freedom and sent him to London where he was finally set free and sent back home to work for the Royal African Company of London in his homeland. While in London he wrote down three copies of the Quran from memory.

He returned home in 1734, as a Royal African Company representative. Job's name in Africa was Ayuba ibn Solomon ibn Ibrahim Jallo (Job son of Solomon son of Abraham Jallo).

Job was the son of an *imam* (leader of the prayer) in Bundu. Reports describe him as a well-mannered, courtly, intelligent, monotheistic, and literate human being who came out of Africa. As a slave he was allowed a place to pray and other conveniences in order to make his slavery as easy as possible. Job was a *hafiz,** who wrote out by hand three copies of the Quran from memory. He was married to two wives before his capture. His first wife was the daughter of the *alpha*** of Tombut and together they had three children Abdullah, Samba, and Ibrahim. Job's second wife was the daughter of the *alpha* of Tomga together they had a daughter named Fatima.

Job was blessed with winning his freedom and returning home to his family. When he returned home, his entire family was still alive and well. Job's life contains many beautiful stories indicating God's blessings and mercy; it

---

* A hafiz is someone who has memorized the entire Qur'an.

** Alpha is a religious leader (imam)

13

contains the story of how a father's love for his son helped to win the son's freedom.

In **1750**, true to legend, the Melungeons were already in the area of Knoxville, TN; Camden, SC; and Marion, NC when the first Europeans arrived.

The tombstone marker of Mahmet, Norwich Connecticut. Photo by Amir Muhammad

In **1750,** in the royal burial ground of the Mohegan Indians in Norwich, CT one of the memorials state "In memory of Elizabeth Joquib, the daughter of Mahomet, great-grandchild to the first Uncas, great sachem of Mohegan, who died July 5th, 1740 aged 38 years old. Mamohet (Mahomet) was the rightful heir of Qwenoco but Ben, the youngest son of Uncas, of illegitimate birth, succeeded Caesar the successor as sachem after Owenoco. (From Indian Races of America / The New England Coast.)

March 3, **1753** Muslims from North Africa, appear in the records of the *South Carolina Council Journal* (no. 21, pt. 1, pp. 298–299), two men by the name Abel Conder and Mahamut (Mahomet) petitioned the South Carolina royal authorities in Arabic for their freedom. They came from Asilah (Sali) on the Barbary Coast of Morroco. Their story is that they were in a battle in 1736 with the Portuguese when they lost and were captured. An officer named Captain Henry Daubrib asked them if they would be willing to serve him for five years in Carolina. When they arrived in South Carolina they were transferred to Daniel LaRoche, who enslaved them for fifteen years until 1753 when they petitioned the authorities for their freedom and won. (From the article "93 Muslim Slaves, Abducted Moors, African Jews, Misnamed Turk," by James Hagy in the *Carologue*, a publication of the South Carolina Historical Society.)

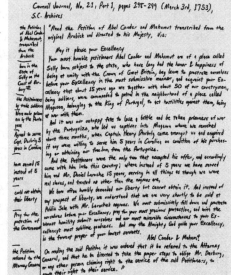

Hand written copy of petition. Courtesy of Sumter Historical Society.

In **1767**, **Kunta Kinte** was captured and enslaved. Kunta Kinte was a Muslim born in 1750, in the village of Juffure in Gambia. He was shipped to Annapolis, Maryland on the ship Lord Ligonier and sold to a Virginia planter. Kunta Kinte fought hard to hold on to his Islamic heritage. Having learned the Qur'an as a boy Kunta scratched Arabic phrases in the dirt and tried to pray every day after he arrived in America. Kunta Kinte was Alex Haley's Mandingo forebearer, who he talks about in his book Roots.

In **1768,** a Muslim living in South Carolina wrote four Surahs from the Quran. He was the slave of Captain David Anderson. There are at least nine different people reported to have written Arabic text during this period.

By **1769,** some of the Muslim runaways were women. One of the first written records of Muslim women was in

15

1769, in the Savannah Georgia Gazette on November 22, 1769. The Gazette advertised about six runaway slaves from the M'Gillivray's plantation at Vale-Royal, GA. They all had just arrived into the country. The women were all from Guinea. Their names were Jamina, a stout woman about 20 years old, Belinda 18 years old, and Hagar around 18 years old. The men were Jacob and Charles from Guinea, and Tony who came from Kishee. They were all around 23 years old.

Savannah Georgia Gazette, September 7, 1774. Supplement.

RUN AWAY from the subscriber's plantation on Augustin's Creek near three years ago, A short well made NEGROE FELLOW, called Mahomet*, hard-favoured, and appears to be pitted with the smallpox, part of one ear is cut off. Such a Negroe as is here described has been seen at a settlement near the Indian Line on Ogechee very lately. Whoever apprehends the said Negroe, and delivers him at the Work House in Savannah, shall receive a reward of ten pounds sterling; and whoever will give information at whose plantation the said Negroe has been secreted for some time past, so as the person who has employed him may be convicted thereof, shall be entitled to a reward of twenty pounds.

From **1774-1775,** many runaway slave advertisements were of Muslim runaway slaves. Like the one in the Savannah Georgia Gazette, in September 7, 1774 for a run away Negro fellow named Mahomet.

Armer was about twenty years old when he ran away from the plantation of Thomas Graves in Richmond county GA. In **April 1789** an advertisement seeking his capture was in the Savannah Georgia Gazette.

Osman was a runaway slave who was met by an artist in Virginia. There is not much known about Osman to date.

In **March 18, 1790,** the Savannah Georgia Gazette advertises about two runaways named Osman and Charles both of a yellow complexion, tall and slim, and around 26 years old from around Dublin, Great Ogechee, GA.

In **May 24, 1775,** the Savannah Georgia Gazette recorded three different **Sambo's.** The first ad was from the plantation of Lachlan M'Gillivray at Vale-Royal which named three Muslims, Quamie about 30 years old, **Sambo** about 22 years old and from the Moorish country, and another **Sambo** about 25 years old. In a second ad from the plantation of Philip Dell was a slave named Sambo about 30 years old and was born in this country.

On June 17, **1775,** Peter (Saleem) Salem born (1750?-1816) a former slave, fought in the Battle of Bunker Hill. The battle was fought at Breeds Hill. According to one story, the colonial troops were near defeat, and British Major John Pitcairn ordered them to surrender. Salem then stepped forward and shot Pitcairn. Pitcairn later died of the wound. Peter Salem got awarded for fighting in the Revolutionary War, and he also fought at Lexington. Peter Salem and Salem (Saleem) Poor were honored for their bravery.

Salem was born enslaved in Framingham, Massachusetts. He had at least two owners in his lifetime. The first owner was Jeremiah Belknap. Belknap sold him to Lawson Buckminister of Framingham. Buckminister allowed Salem to enlist in the colonial army. In exchange for enlisting in the army, Salem received his freedom.

After receiving his freedom "Peter Buckminister" changed his name to Salem. He was also known as "Salem Prince." Local legend has it that the name Salem came from a Massachusetts privateers port where all of the sailors went during the Revolutionary War when people were fighting on their boats. History reports that an old Jewish man told the people that the word was like "shalom" which means peace. The name for peace in Arabic is Salaam and Saleem in Arabic means one who is peaceful.

Salem (Saleem) remained in the army for several years, long enough to fight in the battles of Saratoga and Stony Point. After the war he settled in Leicester, Massachusetts where he barely earned a living weaving cane seats for chairs. He died in the poor house in Framingham in 1816. Postage stamps have been made of Peter Salem and Salem Poor as American Revolutionary war heros.

In **1777,** Morocco becomes the first country to acknowledge America's independence as a new country.

In **1784,** Thomas Jefferson, Benjamin Franklin, and John Adams were commissioned to negotiate a treaty with the Emperor of Morocco.

In **1786,** Morocco became the sixth and the first Muslim country to sign a Peace Treaty with the United States. Algeria in 1795, Tripoli in 1796, Tunis in 1797, and Muscat (Oman) in 1833 followed.

In **1786,** two Muslim men appeared in Charleston, SC "dressed in the Moorish habit" and aroused a great deal of suspicion by their strange ways. An officer of the law attempted to question them and found they were Moors who did not speak English. They were taken to an interpreter who found out they came from Algeria and sailed to Virginia where they had been arrested. Then they traveled overland to South Carolina. (Carologue, a publication of the South Carolina Historical Society 93 Muslim Slaves, Abducted Moors, African Jews, Misnamed Turks by James Hagy.)

In **1787,** the Treaty of Peace and Friendship was signed on the Delaware River between the United States and

Morocco which bears the signatures of Abdel-Khak, Muhammad Ibn Abdullah and George Washington.

In **1788-1789,** The Sultan Mohammed III and President George Washington exchanging letters about peace and asking the Sultan to intercede with authorities in Tunis and Tripoli to obtain the right of free navigation for American ships in the Mediterranean.

Letter from His Majesty Sultan Mohammed III to President George Washington

In the name of God, the merciful. There exists strength and power only by God.

From the Servant of God, Mohammed Ibn Abd Allah may God help him, to the President of the United States of America. Salvation be upon him who follows the Righteous Path.

We received your letter in which you propose a peace* treaty. (We are informing you that) our intention is also to maintain peaceful* relations with you. We have also contacted Tunis and Tripoli regarding what you solicited from Our Majesty** and all requests will materialize, God willing.

Written on the 15 Dhu al-Qa'da 1202 (August 17, 1788)

* At the time this was written, the word "peace" was also used to mean friendship. The Treaty discussed was a friendship treaty.

** Washington had asked the Sultan to intercede with authorities in Tunis and Tripoli to obtain the right of free navigation for American ships in the Mediterranean.

1788 Letter to President George Washington from the Sultan of Morocco.

In **1787** the Baltimore Maryland Journal and the Baltimore Advertiser, advertise two Muslims one named Mingo of yellowish complexion from Baltimore county, and the other named Anthony a dark mulatto around 23 years old from Talbot County. The ad says he has the appearance of an Indian or Moor.

August 20, **1789** the *Savannah Georgia Gazette*, runs an advertisement for a Muslim women runaway describing her as "A Young Negro Wench, named Hagar, has on oznabrig clothes, and wears a handkerchief on her head. She has been seen a day or two ago selling watermelons near town."

In **1788, Abrahim Abdul Rahman ibn Sori** (1762-1829) born in Timbo, West Africa (In present day Guinea) was

19

An engraving of crayon drawing by Henry Inman 1828. From the *Colonizationist and Journal of Freedom* (1834).

captured. He was known as the "Prince of Slaves." He was a Fulbe from the land of Futa Jallon. Abrahim was captured by warring tribes and sold to slave traders in 1788 at the age of 26. He was bought by a Natchez, Mississippi cotton and tobacco farmer, where he eventually became the overseer of the plantation.

Ibrahim Abdul Rahman was a calvary leader who was captured returning home from a successful battle. His homeland was Timbo, (Futa-Jallon) in present day Guinea. He was a Fulbe (Fulani) and lived from 1762-1829. Rahman had been a student in Timbuktu and wrote Arabic after being away for more than thirty years. Rahman ran away for a little while, but returned to his slave master.

Abdul Rahman was seen regularly saying his required prayers five times a day. He was once a leader among the soldiers in Africa, and as a slave he was a slave manager in the Natchez area of Mississippi. Rahman was the sole plantation manager from around 1800-1818.

He impressed blacks and whites from Cincinnati to Boston to Washington, DC with his dignity and piety. He wrote several short pieces for various dignitaries in the United States after a letter of his reached Morocco, which became instrumental in gaining his freedom.

He finally earned his freedom after 40 forty years of slavery, at the age of 66 in 1828. After obtaining his freedom he worked to raise money to ransom his enslaved children's freedom. He and his wife did manage to get to Liberia, where he died before making it back to his actual homeland. About a year later eight of his family members were able to join his wife in Liberia using the funds he had raised.

Ibrahim Abdul Rahman was known as the "Prince of Slaves."

In **1790,** South Carolina passed the Moors Sundry Act which was enacted by the legislative body to grant a special statute for the subjects of the Sultan of Morocco. A group of "Moors" by the names of Francis, Daniel, Hammond, and Samuel, along with their wives, four Muslim women named Fatima, Flora, Sarah, and Clarinda, asked the South Carolina House of Representatives to treat them as free whites. They stated that while they had been fighting for the emperor of Morocco against an African King they had been taken prisoners. A Captain Clark had the Moors delivered to him on the promise he would take them to England where the ambassador from Morocco would purchase their freedom. Instead, Clark brought them to South Carolina where he sold them as slaves. (The Journals of the House of Representatives, 1789-1790.)

In **1790,** Sumter county, the South Carolina census recorded the name Joseph Benenhaly, his Islamic name was Yusef Ben Ali from North Africa. General Thomas Sumter recruited Benenhaly, of Arab descent, and another man known as John Scott to fight with him in the American Revolution. Originally, it is believed that they were pirates. After the war, Sumter took them inland with him to near Stateburg where they settled down and many of their descendants have remained. His dark-skinned descendants, became known as the Turks of Sumter County because of their Moorish background. The Turks claimed the lands along the sourthern coast of the Mediterranean as a part of their empire.

In **1792,** the South Carolina legislature passed a law which stopped the importation of slaves into the state. One provision stated that Moors could not be bound for terms of years of service and could not be brought into South Carolina from other states in the Union either by land or sea. (From the article "93 Muslim Slaves, Abducted Moors, African Jews, Misnamed Turk," by James Hagy in the *Carologue,* a publication of the South Carolina Historical Society.)

During the **1730s** among the Muslims taken into slavery there were at least three who became well known, Job ibn Solomon, Yarrow Mamout, and Lamine Jay. Later in the century came Ibrahim Abdul Rahman known as (The Prince of Slaves), and Mohamet a runaway slave from around Savannah, Georgia.

Later in the **1700s** came Kunta Kinte, Lamen Kebe, Omar ibn Said, Salih Bilali, Bilali known as (Ben Ali, Abu Ali), Charno, Osman, Mohammed Kaba, Mohammed, Samba, Abu Bakr, and Abu Muhammad Abdullah ibn abi Zaid al-Qairawani, to name a few.

Some came from prominent and powerful families. They were teachers, cavalry leaders, religious leaders, and students of law. There are at least seven known Muslim slaves who ran away from their slave masters, three were captured again and two escaped. Some were able to win their freedom back to Africa, others became trusted slave managers.

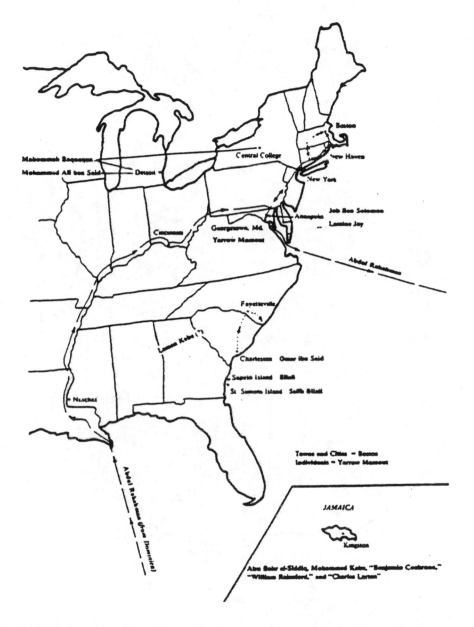

Map I: Known American Homes and Travels of Some Muslims

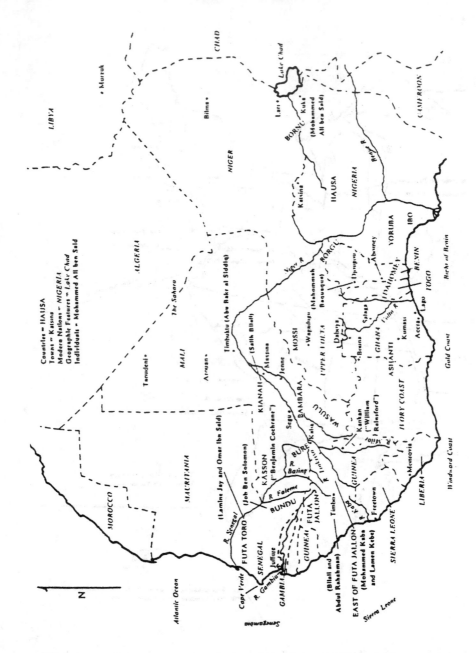

Map II: The Homeland of Captured Muslims

Historical Moments in the 1800s

The 1800s usher in one of America's earliest Muslim communities and cities with Islamic names. Some being founded by Muslims. Muslims fought in the War of 1812 and in the Civil War. Some even became local and regional folk heros.

In 1803, Salih Bilali (Old Tom) came from a powerful family of Massina in the Temourah district in West Africa. He was captured around 1782, sold in the Bahamas at first and then in the US around 1803. He lived from 1770- 1846. He was sold to John Couper in the Bahamas and brought to Saint Simon Island, GA.

From James Prichard, *Illustrations to the Researches into the Physical History of Mankind,* 1844.

From 1816-1840 Salih Bilali was the trusted head slave manager of more than 450 enslaved men and women of John and Hamilton Couper. It was reported by his master's son, that while Salih was on his death bed that his last words were "Allah is God and Mohammed his Prophet."

One of Salih's descendants was Robert Abbott, founder of the "Chicago Defender," one of the nation's first black newspapers. Another one of Salih's descendants was named after him Bilali Sullivan, who was known as (Ben Sullivan). Bilali (Ben) Sullivan purchased some of the original property from the plantation in 1914. He was interviewed about his life in the 1930s.

There are two well known Muslim communities of the Gullah Islands on St. Simon and Sapelo off the coast of

Georgia. Bilali (Ben Ali) Mahomet and Salih Bilali ruled as plantation mangers and Muslim leaders. In America's history there were Gullah Wars. Some of them are known as the Seminole Indians' Wars. The African-American language Gullah was initially developed by the enslaved African Muslims and non-Muslims to help communicate among the various African tribes.

Bilali, sometimes called Bu Allah (Abdullah), or Ben Ali, was a Fula from Timbo Futa Jallon in the highlands of present day Guinea-Conakry. Thomas Spalding of Sapelo Island, GA bought Bilali and his family as slaves from the Bahamas around 1803. Thomas Spalding was a prominent Georgian master, who often wrote for newspapers.

In 1829 Bilali left a 13 page hand written Arabic manuscript, which shows that he was a well-educated man beyond the basic Quranic learning. The arabic letter called a "Risala" talks about some of the laws of Islam and Islamic living. The book is known as Ben Alis' Diary, housed today at the University of Georgia in Athens. His collection had some excerpts from a fairly well-known West African legal text of the Malikite "school of thought" that was predominant in Muslim West Africa, from Morocco to the Gulf of Guinea. Bilali's manuscript has chapters dealing with ablution, the call to prayer, and on a healthy daily life. Bilali's book title translates to mean the "First Fruits of Happiness."

Bilali (Ben Ali) was the leader of one of America's earliest known Muslim communities. He started one of the first Muslim communities in America while still in slavery. Bilali had 12 sons and 7 daughters. Nobody seems to know what happened to his sons. His daughters' names were Margaret, Hester, Charlotte, Fatima, Yoruba, Medina, and Binty (Bint). It is reported that all but Binty could speak English, French, Fulbe, and Arabic. He gave Muslim names and traditions to his nineteen children.

On Sapelo Island, Bilali, was the sole manager and he was directly in charge of more than five hundred of his fellow slaves. He also saved them twice. In 1812 there were at least eighty Muslim men living on the plantation managed by Ben Ali. During the War of 1812, Bilali warned the British that he and eighty of his men would defend the Island with their life and property. Bilali told his master, "I will answer for every Negro of the true faith, but not for the Christians you own." Bilali also became famous for saving them in 1824. When a great hurricane hit Sapelo Island Bilali directed them into the cotton and sugar houses made of an African material, called tabby. Remains of some of these houses are still visible today.

Bilali was known for regularly wearing his fez (Kofi) and a long coat, praying the obligatory prayers facing the east 5 times a day, having his own prayer rug, and for always observing the Muslim fast and feast days (Id) when they came. Bilali was also buried with his Quran and prayer rug.

With Bilali and the presence of many prominent Fulbe people and other Muslims with Islamic manners and culture living among the enslaved West Africans in the south. They help develop and influenced the Gullah culture.

Pages 10 and 11 of Bilali's Arabic-American manuscript. Photo taken from the Georgia State Library, Atlanta.

Tabby houses on Sapelo Island in Georgia built by Bilali and his community*

* Tabby is a mixture of water, lime, sand and sea shells in equal parts.

Picture by Amir Muhammad, 1997: Remains of Tabby houses on Sapelo Island. GA.

Built in the early 1800s, the tabby ruin was once a one and a half story, 10 room hospital for the slaves of Retreat, Georgia, on St. Simon Island, which was under Salih Bilali's control. Photo by Amir Muhammad, 1997.

31

Picture by Amir Muhammad, 1997: Remains of Tabby houses on Sapelo Island. GA.

Picture by Amir Muhammad, 1997: Remains of Tabby houses on Sapelo Island. GA.

In **1807, Yarrow (Mamout) Marmood** was given his freedom. Yarrow was enslaved and brought from Guinea, West Africa before the American Revolution. Yarrow was given his freedom by Upton Beall of Montgomery County, in the Washington, DC area. On April 13, 1807, Upton Beall's deed was recorded and stated that the Negro Yarrow was given his freedom because he was more than forty-five years old and that he would not become a bother to the County of Washington.

Photo by Charles Willson Peale in 1819.

Yarrow (Mamout) Marmood worked out his freedom and became a landowner and a local character in Georgetown in Washington, DC, where he was well known for practicing his Islamic religion publicly.

Yarrow lived to be more than 100 years old. The dates of his birth and death have been record as 1736-1844. Yarrow descended from the Shepherd Kings of Egypt. There are two paintings of him today, one hanging in the Historical Society of Pennsylvania, and the other at the Georgetown Public Library, Washington, DC.

The 1810 census of Washington, DC listed Yarrow Marmood name as only Yarrow and a female living with him, perhaps his wife. In the 1820 census his name was listed as Yarrow Marmood and listed a female still living with him. Yarrow had established a hauling business, owned real estate on what is now 3330-3332 Dent Place NW, and invested some of his savings in the stock of the Bank of Columbia. One of Yarrow's neighbors and friend was another manumitted slave named Joseph Moor who became a respectable grocer in Georgetown.

In Washington, DC the 1820 census identifies Yarrow Marmood and Joseph Moore, both with families and free men. On April 12, 1844, Yarrow's estate was administered by probate court in Washington, DC, under the name Negro Yarrow.

Abraham, an African American Slave of Chief Micanopy.

In **The War of 1812, Abraham** joined the British Colonial Marines who had occupied Spanish Pensacola. Abraham lived from 1787-1870. He was well known as a very gifted individual, soft spoken, and intelligent. Abraham came to Pensacola, Florida sometime in the early 1800s. During his years in Pensacola, Abraham had been a slave of Dr. Eugenio Antonio Sierra, a prominent Spanish physician and surgeon.

He was held in high esteem and worked as an interpreter, for he spoke several different languages. Soon after the Fort Negro construction Abraham left out on his own. He soon gained a reputation as a businessman or a man after profit.

Abraham became involved in trade with the Maroons and the Seminole Indians of the lower Suwannee River area. Gradually, he was accepted by the Maroons and became their foremost leader. The Seminoles had a high regard for Abraham.

Chief Micanopy, the top hereditary chief in the Seminole Nation, appointed Abraham as the "sense-bearer" or legal counsel. As the military leader of the Maroons, he was known by the name "Sounoffee Tustenuggee" which means "Suwannee Warrior." Abraham was married to a woman named Hagar. Abraham and Hagar had two sons named Renty and Washington. Abraham lived peacefully with his family and people in the villa of Pilaklikaha, raising horses, cattle, and growing crops.

After the first Seminole War, Abraham and a delegation of Indian Chiefs went to Oklahoma in 1832 to inspect the land being offered to them in the treaty that was to move them out of Florida. The United States officials would not allow Abraham and the others to leave until they signed the treaty, which they did on March 28, 1833. Abraham opposed the move, therefore spending almost eight months at Fort Gibson. Abraham and several other leaders were opposed to the treaty after learning of its deception, thus the second Seminole War began 1835 to 1842. Abraham had fought in almost every battle of the Seminole Indians' Wars until 1837.

However, in February of 1839 he moved to Oklahoma with his family and became a successful cattle rancher.

In America's history there were Gullah Wars. Some of them are known as the Seminole Indians' Wars.

Abraham returned to Florida in 1852, ten years after the government officially declared an end to the Seminole

35

War. The government hired Abraham to take chief Billy Bowlegs, his father in-law, and some other chiefs to Washington, DC., in order to convince the Indians to leave Florida. They met with Millard Fillmore who became President after Zachary Taylor died. The chiefs still refused to move to Oklahoma. They went back to Florida and disappeared in the everglades. Abraham went back to his ranch in Oklahoma where he died years later, sometime after the Civil War in 1870. He was buried in an unmarked grave in today's Seminole county.

Abraham among the Indians. He is behind the others in the middle of the picture.

Omar ibn (Said) Sayyid 1770-1864, was a Foula. He was taken from a famous Serahule family of teachers, from Fut Tur in present day Senegal. He arrived in America as a slave in 1807, and was shipped to Charleston, SC for a short time, then in 1810 Omar escapes to North Carolina. Omar was married and had a son. He was also a teacher, and studied in Bundu before his capture.

Omar was a descendant from Arabian Muslims who migrated to West Africa in the seventh century. Omar was known as a teacher and saint to a few early ethnologists and African colonizer by 1836.

Omar was given an Arabic written Bible and a Qur'an by his slave master. The Bible is housed today at Davidson College in North Carolina.

Photo courtesy of Davidson University.

Omar was placed on the Owen Hill plantation. While in captivity he ran away from his first slave master, and was later caught and imprisoned in Fayetteville, NC where he persuaded James Owen, a general in the state militia and brother of John Owen, to ransom him for $900, and they treated him gently for the rest of his life. John Owen later became Governor of North Carolina.

Omar lived more than a half a century as a storyteller and an apparent oriental (Muslim) saint to neighbors and visitors from near and far. Omar ibn (Said) Sayyid was called Moreau in slavery. In 1831 Omar wrote a letter to Lahmen (Paul) Kebe and in 1836 the letter was given to Theodore Dwight which contained Omar's autobiography. He also left several short pieces. Most of his papers were prayers from the Bible and the Quran. Omar's friend Kebe wrote him at least once. Omar was still able to write Arabic after thirty years of being enslaved and away from his homeland.

For some time he prayed as required of a Muslim, but he found it polite to pretend to be Christian at times. Omar did not have any more children after he was enslaved.

Omar died in 1864 at the age of 94, he was buried on the Owen Hill plantation in the family burial ground on the plantation.

Omar's 1840 writing of the Psalms found at Davidson College, Davidson, North Carolina. Photo Amir Muhammad: Courtesy of Davidson College.

Omar's writing found at Davidson College, Davidson, NC. Photo Amir Muhammad: Courtesy of Davidson College.

Omar's Arabic Bible given to him by his slave master found at Davidson College, NC. Photo Amair Muhammad: Courtesy of Davidson College.

One of Omar's earliest known writings, 1819. Courtesy of Franklin Trask Library, Andover Newton Theological Seminary, Newton MA.

38

In **1803, Salih Bilali** (Old Tom) came from a powerful family of Massina in the Temourah district in West Africa. He was captured around 1782, sold in the Bahamas at first and then in the US around 1803. He lived from 1770-1846. From 1816-1840 Salih Bilali was the trusted head slave manager of more than 450 slaves of John and Hamilton Couper on St. Simon Island, GA. It's reported that Salih's last words were "Allah is God and Mohammed his Prophet."

In **1805,** a slave named Sambo who knew Arabic had escaped from a plantation on the Ashley River, in South Carolina. The announcement in the Courier on February 9, 1805 offered a reward of $5 for his recovery. It stated that he was about 5' 5", slender body and writes the Arabic language.

In **1807,** Yarrow (Mamout) Marmood was given his freedom. Yarrow was enslaved and brought from Guinea, Africa before the American Revolution.

In **1807,** Hajj Omar Ibn Sayyid was captured at the age of 37. Omar was a Fula born in Fur Tur in present day Senegal. He was born from a Serahule family. Omar lived from 1770-1864. He studied in Bundu, Senegal where he learned how to read and write arabic, Islamic studies, and made Hajj in Mecca before his capture. Omar ibn Sayyid wrote many items in Arabic while enslaved. He wrote the Lords Prayer, the Bismillah, the 23rd Psalm, and others.

In **1808,** a slave named Mustapha, owned by Mathias Sawyer of Edenton, NC was convinced by a white man named Arthur Howe to run away. There plan was to sell and resell Mustapha on their journey northward. After each time Mustapha would escape and team up with Howe again. When they reached Virginia they would depart company and Mustapha could make his way north. Richmond Enquirer, July 8, 1808.

By **1815,** Paul Cuffe, a noted shipbuilder, captain, philanthropist, and nationalist made 18 trips to Africa and in 1815 he took 38 African-Americans back to freedom on his ship in Sierra Leone.. Paul was a descendant of a Muslim family from Ghana. Paul was born in 1759 in Cuttyhunk, Massachusetts. His father's name was Haiz (Saiz) Kofi. Paul Cuffe was the first black to petition the ruling powers of government to free every slave and to allow every colored man desiring to leave America the freedom to do so.

In **1818,** Medina, Ohio was organized. It was originally called Mecca, then later it was changed to Medina, making it the seventh place on the globe at the time called Medina. Three other cities in America bear the name Medina- Medina, New York; Medina, Michigan and Medina, TX.

In **1828,** Abrahim Abdul Rahman ibn Sori (1762-1829) was set free by the order of the Secretary of State Henry Clay and President John Quincy Adams. He was born in Timbo, West Africa (in present day Guinea). He was known as the "Prince of Slaves." Abrahim was a Fulbe from the land of Futa Jallon. Abrahim left Futa in 1774 to study in Mali at Timbuktu.

In **1828,** a Muslim named Sterling living in Hartford, CT met Abdul Rahman during his visit to the New England States.

In **1830,** Charno, a Muslim slave in Georgia, was asked to show his ability to write. He did so by writing nine lines of script from the Qur'an. He wrote out the Al-Fatiha (the opening chapter of the Qur'an). Charno was educated in Africa before his capture. He was among the few slaves who left behind a manuscript. Prior to the Civil War, Charno's literary skills were noticed and quoted on a page of William A. Carruthers' 1834 novel "The Kentuckian," published in New York.

In **1832,** The Village of Mahomet, IL was laid out. Mahomet, IL was originally named Middletown. Sometime during the 1840s it was changed to Mahomet, IL.

In **1834,** A Muslim woman named Sylvia appears in "Knights of the Golden Horseshoe," by William A. Carruthers.

In **1834,** in Tennessee, a Muslim by the name of Hamet Abdul is reported to have sought money to return to Africa.

In **1834,** two Muslims by the names of Jupiter (Dawud) Dawod and Big Jack were reported by the American Colonization Society's "The African Repository" to be well-known slaves in New Orleans. Big Jack was a plantation manager.

In **1835, Lamen Kebe** known as (Old Paul) was liberated after having been in servitude in South Carolina and Alabama. Lamen Kebe was captured in battle and arrived in America in the early 1800s. Lamen returned back to Africa at the age of sixty in 1835.

41

Lamen Kebe arrived in America early in the 1800s. He was from an elite and sophisticated class of Africans who were trained to rule, advise, teach, protect, lead, trade, translate, to go to war, collect taxes, and to travel. Kebe was captured in battle. He was literate, wrote and read Arabic, and prayed to Allah on the Christian slave ship. Kebe came from Senegambia, from a famous Serahule family of teachers. They were the founders of ancient Ghana, who were among the earliest converts to Islam south of the Sahara. His mother was a Manenka.

Kebe decided against bringing children into the world that he had been forced into. In slavery he was known as "Old Paul." He learned in three southern states how ignorant Americans were of Africa. Kebe thru Omar, provided Theodore Dwight, a member of the American Ethnological Society, with information of his native land, the school system there, and how widespread school was among his people. He also named 30 books written by his people.

Photo by Amir Muhammad courtesy of the City of N.Y.

In **1839,** Oman's ruler, Sayyid Sa'id, ordered his ship "The Sultana" to set sail for America on a trade mission. The ship touched port in New York on April 30, 1840. The voyage was not a commercial success. The ship's commander, Ahmed bin Nauman bin Muhsin Al-k'abi Al-Bahraini came from Zanzibar.

Ahmed bin Nauman bin Muhsin Al-k'abi Al-Bahraini's photo hangs today on the third floor of City Hall in New York, NY.

In **1845,** Osman Rockman died. His tombstone was found in Connecticut.

In **1852,** another Osman, known as "General Osman," became the leader of the North Carolina Dismal Swamp com- munity from 1852- 1862. Osman was a runaway slave from

Found by Amir Muham- mad in Windsor, Ct.

Virginia and lived in the dismal swamp. At one time the dismal swamp was partly owned by George Washington, the first President of the United States. The swamp was drudged out by slave labor in the mid-1700s.

Osman, NC by Porte Crayon

In **1856,** The United States cavalry hired a Muslim by the name of Hajj Ali to experiment with raising camels in Arizona. He experimented with breeding camels in the desert. Hajj Ali came from Syria in the mid 1850's. In 1868, Hajj went to work prospecting and scouting for the government. He became a local folk hero in Quartzsite, AZ, where he died in 1902. He was known as "Hi Jolly." His tombstone is a stone built pyramid with a camel on top of it.

Tombstone of Hajj Ali (Hi Jolly)

In **1859,** in Savannah, Ga, many slaves were sold from the Butler plantation in Darien, Ga. Some of the slaves sold were Muslims. It was reported that some of the women wore gorgeous turbans and one of them had a string of beads. At the auction a Muslim named Abel age 19 was sold for $1,295, and one named Hagar, age 50, was sold for $300.

In **1860**, a Muslim lady known as "Old Lizzy Gray" died in Edgefield County. Her obituary, appeared on the front page of the Edgefield Advertiser, on September 12, 1860. Her physician and owner Dr. E.J. Mims wrote that according to the best computations she was 127 years of age. She had four children in Africa before being taken prisoner. During the revolution she was a prisoner on board an English ship. Before her capture she was educated as a Muslim. As a slave she seems to have combined both faiths and became a member of the Methodist Church. She was known to have always said "Christ built the first Church in Mecca."

In **1864**, a monument was erected in New England for a Mr. Smith and it is crowned with three slain Muslim's heads who were slain by Mr. Smith. (From the Isles of Shoals.)

In **1864**, Captain Harry Dean was born. He was the son of Susan Cuffe Dean, whose brother was Paul Cuffe. Captain Dean's family came from Quata, Morocco. For three generations the family were wealthy merchants in Philadelphia. Captain Dean found the first black nautical training school in America. Dean maintained his family's Islamic tradition during his seafaring days on the ship "Pedro Gorino" and in southern Africa where he tried to build an African empire. He was also associated with the Muslim Mosque of London. In the United States he distributed Islamic literature in Chicago, Los Angeles, Seattle, and Washington state.

In **1866**, The Cherokee chief had a Muslim name, Chief Ramadan ibn Wati. Muslims were known to live among many of the different Indian tribes. They lived among the Seminole Indians, The Delawares, The Nanticokes, The Cherokees, and many others.

Mohammed Ali ben Said (1833-1882) known as (Nicholas Said) was born around 1833, and was taken from the heart of Africa around 1850. His family was prominent and he claimed to be the son of Barca Gana, a Bornuese or Bornawa Kashella (General) who was from Bornoo near Lake Chad. He served three masters throughout Libya, Turkey, Europe and parts of Asia.

Picture from Massachusetts Historical Society, Boston

As a traveler's companion, Mohammed made his way to the Caribbean and to North and South America. In 1860 he was offered his freedom and a chance to return to Africa. He decided to go to the U.S. making his way to Detroit and worked as a teacher, and for a few years served as a union soldier.

Mohammed joined the 55th Regiment of Massachusetts Colored Volunteers. Serving in Company 1, Mohammed rose from corporal to sergeant by July 16, 1863.

Later he was reduced from a sergeant at his own request and detailed to a hospital on September 1, 1864 to acquire some medical knowledge. He served for a while in the medical department. Mohammed knew nine different languages, Arabic, Kanouri, Mandara, Turkish, Russian, English, French, German, and Italian. Sometime later he was married and his army records show that he died in Brownsville, Tennessee, in 1882.

In **1869,** a number of Muslims from Yemen arrived in the United States after the opening of the Suez Canal. Most Yemeni's came through New York to Buffalo, and Detroit. Many Yemeni's jumped shipped in San Francisco and settled on the West Coast.

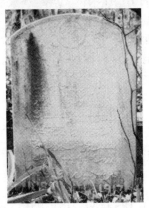

In **1873,** the town of Mecca, Indiana was founded and developed from the Wabash township. The local folk lore states that Arabians founded the town. Mecca has one of the few remaining covered bridges in America. In 1990 the US census records 331 people living in Mecca. Mecca was incorporated as a town in 1970.

Arabic tombstone in the Hixon Cemetery

Mecca, Indiana has two cemeteries located in its' town, one named the Hixon cemetery, the other the Arabian cemetery. In the Hixon cemetery many tombstones were found with the symbol of God's oneness and one written in Arabic in old Turkish script on it of a women related to a Noble Sharif. The US census

Tombstone in the Arabic Cemetery

shows many immigrates from the area came from Eastern Europe or parts of the old Ottoman Empire (Austria, Bulgaria, Hungary, Russia, Slovak).

In **1875,** The first small wave of Muslim immigrants arrived, mainly from Greater Syria (Syria, Lebanon, and Palestine). Some of the Syrian-Lebanese Arabs settled on Manhattan's lower Washington Street and in Brooklyn across the East River around Atlantic Avenue and South Brooklyn. A smaller number came from the Punjab area of India.

Samba Geladio Jegi was best known as Sambo of the American folk tale. In West Africa, Samba (Sambo) means second son.

In **1876,** the Centennial Exposition in Philadelphia attracted Arab merchants and peddlers, where they sold an assortment of merchandise, and some set up centers to import goods.

In **1877,** Seven Algerian escapees from French Guyana were admitted by the Mayor of Wilmington, Delaware, and held as exiles.

Photo by Amir
Muhammad

In **1883,** Sambo Swift died. Born in 1811 he lived as a slave in Darien, Georgia. He was buried as a Muslim with his grave facing northeast and engraved on his tombstone is a hand depicting one finger as the Muslim symbol of the oneness of God. It is believed that Sambo was one of the slaves who were left on the Butlers' plantation at the time of the great sale in 1859. Sambo was a carpenter and had at least three children Abrahim, Mollie and Alonzo.

In **1889**, Edward W. Blyden, a noted scholar and social activist, traveled throughout the eastern and southern parts of the United States proclaiming Islam.

From the mid-1840s to 1914 more than 50 tombstones with the Tawheed (Oneness of God) symbol have been found in Canada and the United States. Found in states from Massachusetts, Connecticut, New Jersey, Maryland, Virginia, North Carolina, Georgia, Michigan, Indiana, to Memphis, Tennessee.

Tombstone found in Richmond, VA.

In **1893,** Mohammed Alexander Russell Webb, became the first known white American convert. Webb lived from 1846- 1916. Webb appeared at the First World Congress of Religions and delivered two lectures: "The Spirit of Islam," and "The Influence of Islam on Social Conditions." He converted to Islam in 1888,

Mohammed was a journalist turned diplomat. Webb was appointed by President Cleveland as the American Consul at Manila, Philippines in 1887.

Webb was an activist for Islam in America, he even found a Mosque in Manhattan, NY which did not last long. He also became the head of the Islamic Propaganda Mission in the US.

Photo Courtesy of Watkinson Library, Trinity College.

In **1897,** Elijah Muhammad was born to a large family in Sandersville, Georgia 1897-1975. He was the leader of the Nation of Islam from 1934-1975. He became a force among poor Blacks and prisoners before becoming a catalyst for contemporary Black political and religious thought.

In 1954 he opened the First Islamic School called the "University of Islam" in Chicago. By 1954 he had more than 50,000 followers. He was a wizard when it came to economics and business.

His "Do for Self" concept of life is often imitated but never duplicated. In December 1959, Mr. Muhammad made the pilgrimage to Mecca.

Historical Moments in the 1900s

Throughout the 80s and 90s the Muslim community has seen much growth. Today Islam is the fastest growing religion in America and has become the second largest relgion in the United States. Today there are many Muslims across the country who are holding elected offices as state representatives, mayors, judges, as well as working for state and local governments. We find Muslims in every profession today as doctors, lawyers, teachers, judges, police officers, and other professions.

From 1900-1917, Wills are found in the Washington, DC Archives beginning with Islamic salutations "With the Name of God Amen" with names like Hannah Henderson, Fontaine Mahmood, James Moore, Mary Newman, Edward Quader, and Anne Yarrow.

In **1902**, twenty families moved from Birey, Syria to Ross, North Dakota.

In **1903**, Mohammed Asa Abu-Howar arrives in New York, then moves to Washington, DC. He becomes a successful builder as A. Joseph Howar, who backed the construction of the Islamic Center.

In **1904**, at the St. Louis Exposition and World Fair merchants and visitors came from the Arab world, at which time an Arab used a waffle to create the first ice cream cone.

In **1905**, The US General Land Office grants land title to one Mahmod Ali.

In **1907**, The Polish Tartars establish "The American Mohammed Society" in Brooklyn, NY.

In **1908**, Muslim immigrants from the Arab provinces of the Ottoman Empire, Syria, Lebanon, Jordan arrive in

North America. They are mainly Turks, Kurds, Albanians, and Arabs.

In **1913**, Noble Drew Ali established the Canaanite Temple in Newark, NJ. The group had some Islamic tendency. They later became "The Moorish Science Temple."

In **1915**, Albanian Muslims in Biddeford, Maine established the first effective Mosque in North America. Most were bachelors working at the Peppermell Mills. Muslim Albanian families still reside in Biddeford and nearby Saco.

In **1919**, the Albanians established another Mosque in Connecticut.

In **1919**, an Islamic association established in Highland Park, Michigan. The organization dismantled after 5 years.

Between **1919-1922,** Islamic associations were formed in Highland Park, MI. in 1919; and in Detroit, Michigan and Brooklyn, N.Y. in 1922.

In **1913**, Noble Drew Ali established the Canaanite Temple in Newark, N.J. Noble Drew Ali was born Timothy Drew, January 8, 1886 on a Cherokee reservation in Sampson, North Carolina. There were immediate challenges to Noble Drew Ali's leadership from within the Moorish community, and by 1916 internal disagreements caused a division of the Moorish-American nation into two groups. One group stayed in Newark, changing its name to the Holy Moabite Temple of the World Moabite, is the ancient name for Moroccans.

Noble Drew Ali and his followers
moved to Chicago in 1925 and established the Moorish Science Temple
of America. By this time, Drew Ali
had established temples in
Charleston, WVA; Milwaukee, WI;
Lansing and Detroit, MI; Philadelphia
and Pittsburgh, PA; Pine Bluff, AR;
Newark, NJ; Cleveland and
Youngstown, OH; Richmond and
Petersburg, VA.

Noble Drew Ali was murdered in
1929 in Chicago, IL and buried in
Burr Oak Cemetery.

Noble Drew Ali

Some early followers of Noble Drew Ali in Newark, NJ. Photo Courtesy of
Michael Nash and James Mendheim Bea

In **1920,** The first Ahmadiyya Muslim missionary to arrive
in America was Dr. Mufti Muhammad Sadiq, who
arrived in Philadelphia on Sunday, February 15, 1920, on
board the Haverford. For religious reasons he was

detained on Ellis Island, New York on February 25, 1920. On May 20, 1920 he was released by the order of the Secretary of the State. Dr. Sadiq stayed in New York for some time and continued to preach Islam. Later, he moved to Chicago and in 1921 established the first headquarters of the Ahmadiyya Muslim Community, at 4448 Wabash Avenue, giving it the name "Al Masjid."

Many of the early Muslim Jazz musicians were first Ahmadiyya, such as Art Blakey, Talib Ahmad Dawoud, Ahmad Jamal, Yusef Lateef, Mohammed Sadiq, Sahib Shihab, Dakota Staton (Aliyah Rabia), McCoy Tyner (Sulieman Saud), and Idrees Sulieman, to name a few.

In **1920,** the Red Crescent, a Muslim charity modeled after the International Red Cross, is established in Detroit.

In **1922,** an Islamic association was established in Detroit, Michigan.

By **1923,** Hassen Mohamed became a successful businessman in downtown Belzoni, Mississippi. He had a general merchandise store. Hassen settled in the Belzoni area in 1911. He came from the Lebanese Shiite village of Sir'een. Hassen was married to Ethel Wright. Together they had eight children. One of their sons Ollie Mohamed became a State Senator. Hassen passed away in 1965.

In **1925,** a Muslim group in Michigan City, Indiana purchased land designated as their cemetery. In the thirties, these Muslims added a Mosque/Community Center. The building is still in use.

In **1926,** Duse Muhammad Ali (1866-1945), mentor of Marcus Garvey, helped establish an organization in Detroit known as the "Universal Islamic Society." Its motto was "One God, One Aim, One Destiny." He was born in Alexandria, Egypt, the son of a Sudanese mother and an Egyptian army officer. He was brought to London at a young age by one of his fathers' friends. He was known to be frequently in the company of Muhammad Pickthall, the English Muslim scholar who translated the Holy Qur'an into English. Duse Ali had considerable influence upon Garvey when they worked together in London, where Duse Ali was the Editor of the African Times and Orient Review.

In **1926,** Polish speaking Tartars opened a Mosque in Brooklyn, NY. In the 1900s Polish Muslims came to Brooklyn, NY. In 1931 they purchased a New England church-style meeting hall and an adjacent three-story residential building which is still in use today. The community is made up of Asian Tartars whose nomadic ancestors helped Vitautas, Grand Duke of Lithuania, in his victory against the Teutonic Order in 1410. They settled in Lithuania and Poland with the status of nobility, while remaining Muslim. They were nearly annihilated during World War II.

In **1928,** The Islamic Propagation Center of America opened up on State Street in Brooklyn, New York, under the leadership of Sheikh Al-Haj Daoud Ahmed Faisal. He also started the Islamic Mission Society which was active from 1934-1942. Sheikh Faisal was granted a charter by Sheikh Khalid of Jordan and King Saud of Saudi Arabia to propagate Islam in America.

57

In **1928,** The early beginnings of the first Mosque of Pittsburgh were rooted in Noble Drew Ali's teaching. Several years after its foundation, the main teacher of the community, Walter Smith Bey, invited Dr. Yusef Khan, an Ahmadi, to speak to and teach the community. During this time of growth and development by 1935 there emerged a new conflict pertaining to Dr. Khan's teachings. Most of the community members concluded against Dr. Khan and the community divided for a second time. Today the community follows the sunnah of the Prophet Mohammed.

In **1929,** Muslim farmers built one of America's first Mosque (Masjid) in Ross, North Dakota. The homesteader Hassen Juma had settled there with 160 free acres in 1899. By 1902, twenty families had followed his path from Birey, Syria. The U.S. objected to their naturalization until 1909 when it withdrew the ban and the Syrians began claiming citizenship. Many fought and died in the two World Wars.

In **1929,** the community built a Mosque, and performed Jum'ah (Friday) prayer service. The farmhouse / mosque was destroyed in 1978. The cemetery on its grounds remains and there is an arched gate with a crescent and star on it.

From: *A Century of Islam in America.* Photo courtesy of Attiyeh Foundation, Washington, DC.

In **1929,** "The Lost-Found Nation of Islam in the Wilderness of North America" was founded by W.D.Fard in Detroit. Fard was known as (Wali D. Fard, Wallace Fard, and W.F. Muhammad). The Nation of Islam was an indigenous African American Islamic expression founded by Wali Fard Muhammad and developed by Elijah Muhammad.

In **1934,** The Muslim community of Cedar Rapids, Iowa built the first Masjid (Mosque) specifically designed as a Masjid. Today the Mosque is known as the "Mother "Mosque." The earlier community was predominantly Lebanese under the leadership of Abdullah Ingram. Cedar Rapid's community has grown and has been able to maintain their Islamic identity.

Photo from *Fifty Years of Islam in Iowa, 1925–1975.*

In **1934,** Elijah Muhammad became the leader of "The Lost-Found Nation of Islam in the Wilderness of North America" which later became known as "The Nation of Islam." The Honorable Elijah Muhammad built a mulitmillion dollar empire by the time of his passing. The Nation of Islam developed many Temples of Islam, and the University of Islam, along with businesses, farms, property, rental property, transportation fleets and more. He produced many great leaders like Al-Hajj Malik El-Shabazz (Malcolm X), Muhammad Ali, Imam W. Deen. Mohammed and Louis Farrakhan.

The Nation of Islam helped change the spelling of Arabic words already in use in the English language to correctly represent their Arabic pronunciation and spelling-

Examples: Moslem to Muslim, Mahomet to Muhammad, Koran to Quran, and so forth.

In **1934,** The First Mosque of Cleveland was a major community of Ahmadiyyas headed by Wali Akram from 1934-1937. By the 1940s there were two hundred people in the Masjid. The community now follows the sunnah or orthodox Islam.

In **1930,** eighteen Muslim slaves were turned up by the Georgia Writers Project, a Works Progress Administration program which collected stories of living ex-slaves in Georgia.

Hajji Wali Akram, Photo by Jolie Stahl

In the **1930's,** three other Mosques (Masjids) were started in Dearborn, MI., Sacramento, CA., and Michigan City, MI.

In the late **1930s,** "The Addeynu Allah Universal Arab Association" a Sunni community was established in Newark, NJ under the leadership of Professor Ezeldeen, who was second in command in Noble Drew Ali's movement and was known as Brother Lomax Bey. He was one of the first African-Americans to master the Arabic language and to go abroad to study Islam in Egypt. He developed orthodox Islamic communities in several cities throughout the United States. Professor Ezeldeen was responsible for establishing the first National Islamic

Professor Ezeldeen

Organization among the Sunni Muslims called "United Islamic Communities," which included Sheikh Daoud, members of the First Mosque of Cleveland and Pittsburgh, along with others.

In **1939,** The Islamic Mission Society is founded in New York by Sheikh Dawud.

In **1940,** The first official Nation Of Islam Temple #4 in Washington, DC was setup by Elijah Muhammad. Three other cities had Temples in Detroit, MN #1, Chicago, IL #2, and Milwaukee, WN #3.

In **1941,** The FBI begins its' program of harassment on the members of the Nation of Islam.

In **1942,** John Ben Ali Haggin, known as Captain Johnny Haggin, became famous for his valor as the pilot of the famous submarine sinking flight, off the coast of New Jersey. John Ben Ali Haggin was born of Irish-Arabian descent on August 19, 1916, in New York City

In **1942,** The Nation of Islam brothers begin preaching in the US prison systems in Petersburg, VA. William X Fagin, Harry X Craighhead, and Benjamin X Mitchell. In Benjamin Mitchell's book he states that "Inmates began to ask us questions about our religion. The three of us began to explain to the inmates the teachings of Islam."

In **1945,** African American Muslims purchase a building and establish the First Muslim Mosque of Pittsburgh, PA. They were the first Mosque to be chartered by indige-nous Muslims in the USA.

In **1946,** the first "The Young Muslim Women's Association" was chartered in Pittsburgh, PA. They had a sub-charter in Missouri that provided services like aid to dependent children, widows, and elders.

In **1946,** The Nation of Islam bought it's first Temple called Temple #2 in Chicago, Illinois.

From **1947-60,** A third wave of Muslim immigrants came from Palestine, Yugoslavia, Lebanon and Egypt.

In **1949,** The Albanian-American Muslim Center of Harper Wood, MI was founded by Imam Vehbi Ismail.

Albanian American Muslim Center

In the **1950s,** a few jazz musicians became Muslims. Art Blakey, Talib Daoud, Mohammed Sadiq, Sahib Shihab, Ahmad Jamal, Dakota Staton, Yusef Lateef, Idrees Sulieman, and McCoy (Sulieman Saud) Tyner, to a name a few.

In **1950,** the first mosque in the nation's capital is established as the "American Fazl Mosque" at 2141 Leroy Place, Washington, DC. It served as the Headquarters of the Ahmadiyya Muslim Community from 1950-1994.

In **1952,** Muslim service men sue the federal government and were allowed to identify themselves as Muslims.

In **1954,** The Federation of Islamic Associations (FIA) of the US and Canada was established.

In **1955,** The State Street Masjid in New York City was established by Sheikh Dawud Ahmed Faisal. It is still in use today. From this Masjid came the Dar-ul-Islam Movement in 1962.

In **1955,** A Mosque was established by Yugoslavians in Chicago. These Muslims arrived in the early 1900s and have evolved into an organized ethnic group with several institutions, including the Bosnian-American Cultural Association.

In **1956,** El-Hajj Malik Shabazz (Malcolm X) (1925-1965), becomes an active preacher for the Nation of Islam. While in prison, he was introduced to Elijah Muhammad's teaching.

In **1957,** The Islamic Center of Washington, DC opened on June 28th 1957. The center was the first one built with a traditional Islamic architect structure. President Dwight Eisenhower gave the opening remarks at the Islamic Center.

In **1960,** Masjid Muhammad of Washington, DC was built as the first Mosque of the NOI under the leadership of Elijah Muhammad.

In **1962,** The first Muslim American Newspaper "Muhammad Speaks" is launched. It later became the largest minority weekly publication in the country and reached more than 800,000 readers at its peak. It has undergone various name change's such as Bilalian News, The American Muslim Journal, to its current name Muslim Journal.

In **1962,** the beginning of Darul-Islam under the leadership of Imam Yahya Abdul Karim, Ishaq A Shaheed, and Rajab Mahmu began in Brooklyn, NY. In the 80s the community came under the influence of Shaykh Jaylani, and many in the community rejected his teachings, eventually pledging allegiance to the leadership of Imam Jamil Al-Amin.

In **1963,** The Muslim Student Association (MSA) was founded. It was organized to aid foreign Muslim students attending schools in the United States. MSA now has more than 150 branches nationwide.

In the **1960s,** the largest Sunni Muslim community of African-Americans was centered in Brooklyn, NY. Shaykh Daoud and Malcolm X both had their Masjid in Brooklyn, NY.

Between **1960s-1980,** a fourth wave of Muslim students and immigrants came to America from all over the Muslim world.

Malcolm and Muhammad Ali after the 1964 Liston fight.

In **1964,** Clarence 13X founded the Five Percenters, after leaving the Nation of Islam in New York. Many rap groups and singers identify with the Five Percenters. Clarence 13x was killed in 1969.

In **1964,** Muhammad Ali, the three time boxing champ of the World won his first heavy weight championship fight beating Sonny Liston. By late 1965 Muhammad Ali made the name "Muhammad" a household name in America. Ali has become an American hero for standing for his beliefs.

In **1965,** Internationally known Muslim leader El-Hajj Malik el-Shabazz (Malcolm X) was assassinated in New York. Malcolm had six children. He left the Nation of Islam in March 1964 and formed a new organization called Muslim Mosque, Inc. In May 1964, Malcolm came back from Hajj in Mecca changing his name to El-Hajj Malik el Shabazz.

Photo: Gannett Rochester Newspaper

In **1967,** the Ansaru Allah community was organized in New York. As Syyid Isa Al Haadi Al Mahdi is the founder of the organization, which changed its name a few times first as "Ansar Pure Sufi," then "Nubian Islamic Hebrews." Isa was born in 1945 in Omdurman, Sudan. Shaykh Daoud was one of Isa's mentors.

In **1968,** The Hanafi Movement is founded by Hamas Abdul-Khaalis. The Hanafi Madhab Center was established in New York but later moved to Washington, DC. At its' peak the community had a membership of more than 1,000 in the United States, which included Kareem Abdul-Jabbar, the famous basketball player.

In **1968,** Islamic Circle of North America (ICNA) was formed as Halaqa Islami of Shumali America. Brothers from South Asia who had experience working with Islamic movements established the organization. Initially the focus was on the immigrant Muslim community of South Asia and the work was done in Urdu language. By the late 1970s, after a major debate it was decided that the organization would work as a grass-root-workers-based Islamic movement of North America. The name ICNA was adopted and the medium of communication was changed from Urdu to English. ICNA established several pioneer institutions: ICNA Relief/Helping Hand, Sound Vision, MSI Financial Services and the Message magazine are some of them.

From **1970-1973,** Dr. Fazlur Rahman Khan, a Muslim from Bangladesh, designed Chicago's John Hancock Center in (1970), the One Shell Plaza in Houston (1971), and the Sears Towers in Chicago in (1973).

In **1972,** the Honorable Elijah Muhammad opened a $2 million Mosque and school in Chicago.

In **1974,** The Muslim World League was granted non-governmental organizational status at the United Nations.

Imam W.D. Mohammed

In **1975,** Elijah Muhammad, the leader of the Nation of Islam, dies February 25th.

In **1975,** Warith Deen Mohammed born 1933, became the leader of the Nation of Islam. He moved the Nation of Islam from nationalism into the Sunnah (orthodox) way of Al-Islam and in 1985 he decentralized the Nation.

66

Under his leadership the community made many positive transitions and name changes from "The World Community of Islam in the West" 1976-81, to "The American Muslim Mission" 1981-85, then "The Ministry of W.D. Mohammed" 1985-97, and currently the "Muslim American Society" 1997. Mr. Muhammad is well known as the Muslim American Spokesman for Human Salvation. He is credited with influencing the African American leadership to change from being called Blacks in America to be called African-Americans.

In **1978,** Imam Warith Deen Mohammed is named as consultant/trustee by the Gulf States to distribute funds for Islamic missionary activities in the U.S.

In **1978,** Minister Louis Farrakhan re-establishes the old Nation of Islam and its' unorthodox teaching.

In **1981,** the first Islamic library was established in Plainfield, IN.

In **1981,** the American Islamic College was founded in Chicago, IL.

In **1981,** the International Institute of Islamic Thought (I.I.I.T.), an American social science organization was founded in Herndon, VA.

In **1982,** the Islamic Society of North America (ISNA) was established as an umbrella organization seeking to meet the needs of both the transient students and resident American Muslims. ISNA is headquartered in Plainfield, IN.

In **1985,** Warith D. Mohammed decentralizes the Nation of Islam.

In **1985,** the Muslim League of Voters (MLV) was established in Irvington, New Jersey. The purpose of M.L.V. is to establish and promote political and economic dignity.

In **1990,** the American Muslim Council (AMC) was established in Washington, DC. AMC is one of the leading Muslim political organizations in the United States serving the Muslim community.

In the early **1990s,** Alim Fatah, a Somalian born Muslim working as an employee for the US Post office, invented the new self adhesive stamp.

In **1991,** Imam Siraj Wahhaj, became the first Muslim in U.S. history to offer the invocation (opening prayer) to the United States Congress House of Representatives.

In **1991,** Charles Bilal, of Kountze, Texas, became the nation's first Muslim mayor in an American city.

In **1992,** Imam Warith Deen Mohammed became the first Muslim in U.S. history to offer the invocation (opening prayer) to the United States Senate.

In **1993,** a National Shura Council was established which comprised of the four national organizations: the Ministry of Imam W.D. Mohammed, Islamic Society of North America (ISNA), the National Community of Imam Jamil Al-Amin, and Islamic Circle of North America (ICNA). A declaration was signed during a seminar organized by the Islamic Resource Institute in Los Angeles, California. It was signed by Imam W.D. Mohammed, Dr. Imtiaz Ahmad, President of ISNA, Imam Jamil Al-Amin, and Dr. Zahid Bukhari, Secretary General, INCA.

In **1993,** Captain Abdul Rasheed Muhammad became the First Muslim Army Chaplin (Imam) in the U.S. Army to be installed. In 1991 according to the United States Department of Defense, there are more than 5,000 Muslims in uniform on active duty in the military.

In **1994,** Council on American-Islamic Relations (CAIR) is established. CAIR has become one of America's leading Islamic human and civil rights organization.

In **1994,** Abdul-Hakeem Muhammad, a Computer Scientist with the IRS, became the first Muslim to win the "Department of the Army Commander's Award for Civilian Service," for his work in the field of computers open systems standards and technical architectural environment. This is one of the highest, rare, and unusual Congressional awards won by an IRS employee. The award was presented by President Clinton's Cabinet appointee Dr. Wushow Chou, Treasury, Deputy Assistant Secretary for Information Systems.

In **1996,** Monje Malak Abd Al-Muta' Ali ibn Noel, Jr. became the first Muslim Naval Chaplin (Imam) in the U.S. Navy.

In **1996,** The American Muslim Council sponsored the first Iftar dinner celebration on Capitol Hill.

In **1996,** The White House hosts its' first Eid reception. The first lady, Hillary Rodham-Clinton recognized the end of Ramadan by hosting a group of Muslim families at the White House reception for Id Al-Fitr.

In **1998,** the U.S. Capitol began conducting Jumu'ah (the Muslim prayer service) every Friday. Another historical first for Muslims in America.

In **1999,** The first New York Police Department Muslim Chaplain was appointed, Imam Izak-El M. Pasha.

August 17, 1999, Osman Siddique was sworn in as U.S. Ambassador to the Fiji Islands. Ambassador Siddique emigrated from Bangladesh and is the first Muslim ambassador to be posted to a foreign country.

USA Postage Stamp

In **1999,** The U.S. Post-office published a stamp to honor the Muslim leader El-Hajj Malik el-Shabazz (Malcolm X). There are two other postage stamps honoring achievements of African-Americans with Islamic roots, Revolutionary War heros Peter (Salem) Saleem and Saleem (Salem) Poor.

In **1999,** the Secretary of State Madeleine K. Albright hosted the first Iftar dinner in US history held by the State Department for Muslim Americans.

By the end of the 20th century Muslims and the religion of Al-Islam have become the fastest growing religion and community in America and has become the second largest religion in the United States. At the beginning of the century there were from 5,000 to 10,000 Muslims living in the United States. Today there are more 6 million Muslims living in the United States with more than

1,000 documented Masajid (Mosques) and Islamic Centers. There are five cities with more than 20 Masajid and Islamic Centers each in them, Houston, TX -31, Brooklyn, NY -25, Detroit, MI -24, Chicago, IL -24, and Philadelphia, PA -20.

Some of America's Islamic leaders at the first Iftar dinner at the State Department.

Today there are many Muslims across the country who are holding elected offices as local City Council members, State Representatives, a Mayor, and Judges. We find Muslims in every profession today as Doctors, Lawyers, Teachers and others.

July 2000, Hassan El-Amin was appointed as a District Judge in Prince George County, Maryland. There are at least two other Muslim Judges in the country David Shaheed of Gary, Indiana and one female Judge Zakia Mahasa, Master Chancery in the family Division of the Baltimore City, MD Circuit Court.

December 2000, the U.S. Postal Service unveils an Eid Stamp which is part of the "Holiday Celebrations" series of the U.S. Postal Service.

The Stamp was designed by calligrapher Mohamed Zakariya.

71

Muslims in Art, Entertainment, Sports, and Personalities

Muslims In Sports

Muhammad Ali, one of the most famous and recognized Muslim personalities in the world this century, three time World Heavyweight Champion, is well known as the people's champ and a strong Muslim. Other boxers who were Muslims during part of their careers are Saad Muhammad, Eddie Mustafa, Dwight Braxten (Muhammad Qawi-Ali), and now Mike Tyson.

Kareem Abdul-Jabbar, a member of basketball Hall-of-Fame, is one of the greatest basketball players of all times. He played for the L.A. Lakers. Other famous Muslim basketball players are Jamal Wilkes, of the LA Lakers; Walt Hazzard, of the Atlanta Hawks; Charlie Scott (Shaheed Abdul-Aleem), of the Phoenix Sun; and Spencer Haywood, of the Phoenix Sun.

Today we have basketball great Hakeem Olajuwon, of the Houston Rockets; Mahmoud Abdul-Rauf, of the Denver Nuggets; Shareef Abdur-Rahim, of the

Vancouver; Larry Johnson, of NY Knicks; Tariq Abdul-Wahad, of Sacramento Kings; and Craig Hodges.

Ahmad Rashad, former receiver for the Minnesota Vikings, now a national sportscaster; Abdus-Salaam, former tackle for the New York Jets; Raghib (Rocket) Ismail, receiver for L.A. Raiders; Salaam a running back for Chicago Bears; Karim Abdul Jabbar, of the Miami Dolphins; Efram Salaam, of the Atlanta Falcons; and Mustapha Muhammad of the Colts are just a few of the many outstanding athletes who are Muslim. There are also many outstanding Muslim athletes in College today.

Muslims in Art and Entertainment

There have been many Muslim entertainers in Jazz like, Jazz great Art Blakey, the Islamic name Blakey chose for himself was Abdullah Ibn Buhauna, McCoy Tyner (Sulieman Saud), Pharaoh Sanders, Ahmad Jamal, Yusef Lateef, Talib Ahmad Dawoud, Dakota Staton (Aliyah Rabia), Mohammed Sadiq, Sahid Shihab, Idris Muhammad, Billy Higgins (Abdullah

Najee Rashid

Karim), Jack McLean (Omar Karim), Idrees Sulieman, Kenny Clarke (Liaqat Ali Salaam), Oliver Mesheux (Mustafa Dalil), Roshann Roland Kirk, Jamal Nasser, Najee, Nasar Abadey drumer, Talib Kibwaye, Sabu Daoud Adeola bass with Ahmed Jamal, and South African born Abdullah Ibrahim.

In the late 1940s, Blakey used his house as a center for Islamic meetings. Yusuf Lateef, converted to Islamic in 1948 during one of these meetings. After the 1960s, the

Nation of Islam became dominant among African-American jazz musicians like Larry Young (Khalid Yasin) and Max Roach.

R&B song writer and producer Muhammad Luqman Abdul-Haqq (Kenny Gamble) of the writing team Gamble/Huff was responsible for the Philadelphia Sound of the late 60s thru the early 80s. Many famous songs sung by the Philly artists had Islamic influence like, "Give the People What They Want," "Together," "Love Train," "Unity," "Family Reunion," "Survival," "You Can't Hide from Yourself," and "Message in Our Music."

Luqman Abdul-Haqq (Kenny Gamble)

Some of the Muslim R&B artists are Khalis Bayyan (Ronald Bell), Amir Abdul-Salaam Bayyan (Kevin Bell), and Muhammad (Kool) Bayyan from the music group Kool and the Gang, Abdul-Aziz (Joe Tex), Abdul Takir member of the Four Tops Motown hall of fame group, Talib Muhammad (Ted Miller) former lead singer of Blue Magic, William Hart of the Delfonics, Mark Greene the original lead singer of the Moments, Motown group "The Boys," Wyclef of the group Fugees, and Wali Ali guitarist and singer.

Islamic influence has been in rap music from the beginning with The Last Poets known as the original rap group. Others are members of the group called Tribe, Groove Theory, Ever last, Q-Tip, Lakim Shabazz, and some members of the rap group Public Enemy, Reggae artist Jimmy Cliff, and pop star Yusuf Islam (Cat Stevens).

77

Muslims in Art and Entertainment

Many Muslims are producers and executives in the music and entertainment business, like Abdul Jalil of Super Star Management, Qasim Ahmed Creative Entertainment, and Royal Bayyan a record executive, to name a few.

Muslim actors, writers, and producers like Moustapha Akkad the producer of The Message, Lion of the Desert, The Story of Islam, and the blockbuster hit Halloween; and Luqman Al-Ghazali aka Ernest Thomas (Roger of What's Happening). Actor Omar Epps comes from a Muslim family, also world renowned model/actor Imani.

Askia Muhammad Toure (Rolland Snelling) is well known as a poet and played a very important role in the development of Black Arts in the 60s and 70s.

Eugene Majeed, is a well known Muslim illustrator whose work reflected the spiritual and metaphysical wisdom of the Muslim African-American community of the late 1960s and early 1970s.

Mohamed Zakariya, is a world renowned calligrapher. His work is exhibited and sold throughout the world. Mohamed is the first American to receive a diploma from the Research Center for Islamic History, Art, and Culture in Istanbul, Turkey. Mohamed is the artist who designed the Eid Stamp for the U.S. Postal Service in 2000.

78

Muslims in the Social Arena

Nobel Drew Ali started the Moorish Science Temple in 1913-29. The Honorable Elijah Muhammad was the leader of the Nation of Islam from 1934-75. Malcolm X (El-Hajj Malik al-Shabazz) was a strong Muslim leader from 1956-65. These men were great leaders and influenced hundreds of thousands of people both Muslim and non Muslim. They helped reform and educate many poor and unlettered people. Like great physicians, their impact is felt even today.

Imam Warith Deen Mohammed is the current leader of the largest indigenous Muslim community in America whose leadership has grown world wide. Many members of his community are known as Bilalians instead of African-Americans, to reflect their Islamic and African cultural history.

Dr. Sayyid Syeed, is Secretary General of (ISNA) Islamic Society of North America, which is one of largest Islamic organization in North America.

Other renowned leaders are Jamil Al-Amin (H. Rap Brown), Siraj Wahhaj, Dr. Naim Akbar, Dr. Khalid Abdullah Tarik Al-Mansur, and the NOI leader Louis Farrakhan.

Betty Shabazz was a woman whose example of courage, compassion and dignity will be an inspiration to many.

Shabazz was known as an educator, college administrator, child advocate, civil rights leader, widow, mother, and keeper of Malcolm X's legacy.

Bogdan Ataullah Kopanski, a Polish-American with a Ph.D. in History and Politics embraced Islam in 1974.

Maryam Jameelah (Margaret Marcus) was born Jewish. She is best known as an essayist, journalist, and author of many books.

Dr. Syed Eqbal Hasan, professor of geosciences and director of the University of Missouri's Center for Applied Environmental Research Department, received the 1999-2000 Educator's Environmental Excellence Award from the US (EPA).

Muslims in Politics

The first recorded Muslim political activity was in 1753 when Abel Conder and Mahamut petitioned the South Carolina House of Representatives for their freedom and won.

In 1991, Charles Bilal of Kountze, Texas became the nation's first Muslim mayor in an American city.

There are many elected Muslim officials around the country. Some are, Larry Shaw, State Senator of North Carolina; Yusuf Abus Salaam, City Councilman of Selma, Al; Lateefah Muhammad, City Councilwoman of Tuskegee, Al. the first elected Muslim woman; Yusuf Abdul-Hakeem, City

Councilman and President of Chattanooga, Tenn.; Nasif Rashad Majeed City Councilman of Charlotte, NC; Bilal Beasley City Councilman and President of Irvington, NJ.; Jimmy Small Salaam, Councilman of East Orange, NJ. Oscar Brooks, Council member of Pemberton Township in New Lisbon, NJ; John Rhodes, Councilman of North Las Vegas, NV; Natalie Bayton, Councilwoman of Oakland, CA; Benjamine Ahmad, Councilman of Menlo, CA; and Suzanne Sareni, Councilwoman of Dearborn, MI.

In 2000, a Pakistan-American, Mr. Saghir Tahir was elected as a State Assembly member of New Hampshire in November.

Ambassador Osman Siddique was the first Muslim ambassador to be posted to a foreign country.

There are many Muslims who are appointed officials all around the country.

Over the years many Islamic political organizations have been formed. One such organization Muslim Public Affairs Committee (MPAC), which is headed by Dr. Maher Hathout.

Conclusion

Islam has survived in many ways and has grown into the fiber of the American society against extreme odds. In the New World, the African slaves, in some cases, suffered a doubly tragic fate. They were enslaved because they were African, but when it was discovered that in addition to being African they were also Muslim, their suffering was often compounded. They were tortured, burnt alive, hung or shot unless they renounced their religion, their names, and accept to be called by the name of the one who claimed to own them. Its been documented that between 10% to 25% of the enslaved Africans brought to the U.S. were Muslims. The reasons why so few of the Africans brought to the U.S. were Muslim was that many of the tribes along the coast where the slave trade was most entrenched were still pagan, although living in empires controlled by a Muslim aristocracy. Documented cases of enslaved African Muslims show that they had originally come from the interior regions of the Islamic empires of Songhai, Ghana, and Mali around areas like Timbuktu.

The earliest Muslim community in the US should be remembered for its strong devotion to Islam under such conditions. The social life and language of the direct descendants of the first documented Muslim community formed the inspiration of the Gullah* language and culture which was initially developed by enslaved African Muslims and non Muslims from Senegal, and Ghana to facilitate communications among the various tribes. Some of the words still generally used today, especially in the south; are Goober (peanut), Gumbo (okra), Ninny (female breast), Tote (to carry), and Yam (sweet potato), and names like Bobo (one who cannot talk), Geeji (a language and tribe in Liberia), Agona (a country in Ghana), Ola (that which saves), Samba (name given the second son (Hausa), and Zola (to love). These names and words come from the influence of African Muslims.

Muslims have contributed to the Western world many Arabic words found in the English language today, such as admiral, algebra, amber, atlas, banana, cable, camel, checkmate, coffee, cotton, jasmine, lemon, magazine, mask, musk, rice, sofa, sugar, syrup, and zero, to name a few.

As Western society moves closer to understanding the diversity of its culture, Islam takes its rightful place in the history of our great nation. We cannot properly identify the full history of America without including the Muslim American. Steadily historians are uncovering the complex threads of America Islamic history to satisfy our brother and sisters lost souls and stories. My present work hopes to unravel some of that history covered up by years of depletion from American history.

Reference Material

Haddad, Yvonne Y. "A Century of Islam in America." In *Islamic Affairs Programs*. 1986.

Curtin, Philip. *Africa Remembered: Narratives by West Africans from the Slave Trade*. Madison, WI, 1968.

McCloud, Aminah Beverly. *African American Islam*. Routledge, NJ, 1995.

Austin, Allan. *African Muslims in Antebellum America: A Source Book*. New York, 1984.

Ferris, Marc. *American Legacy; America's First Black Muslims*. 1997.

Hagy, James. "Muslims Slaves." *Carologue* (South Carolina Historical Society) Spring, 1993.

Windley, Lathan. *Georgia and Maryland Runaway Slaves Advertisements,* n.d.

Koszegi, M. and J. Gordon Melton. *Islam in North America (A Source book)*. Garland Publishing, 1992.

Rashad, Adib. *Islam, Black Nationalism & Slavery (A Detailed History)*. Beltsville, MD: Printers, Inc., 1995.

Numan, Fareed. *The Muslim Population in the United States*. Washington, DC: The American Muslim Council, 1992.

Abdul-Khaliq, Salim. *The Untold Story of Blacks in Islam*. U.B. & U.S. Communications Systems, 1994.

Brandon Institute. *Muslims in Georgia: A Chronology & Oral History*. 1993.

What Became of the Slaves on a Georgia Plantation: A sequel to Mrs. Kemble's Journal. 1863.